AI in Cybersecurity for SMBs

Simplifying Cyber Risk: AI Tools and Tactics for Small Business Survival

Written by
Eric LeBouthillier

AcraSolution | 2025 1st Edition
www.acrasolution.com

Preface

Cybersecurity is no longer a luxury or a technical afterthought — it's a business imperative. In today's rapidly evolving digital landscape, small and medium-sized businesses (SMBs) face the same sophisticated cyber threats as Fortune 500 companies — but without the budget, team, or tools those giants rely on.

At the same time, artificial intelligence (AI) has moved from buzzword to battlefield essential. What once felt like science fiction is now embedded in everything from phishing scams to ransomware — and in the very tools that can help defend against them. The challenge for SMBs isn't whether to adopt AI in their cybersecurity strategy, but how to do it **smartly, affordably, and effectively**.

In this book, you'll learn how to:

- Understand what cyber risk really looks like for your business
- Identify the assets, systems, and data most vulnerable to attack
- Spot emerging threats — including AI-generated attacks
- Leverage low-cost or free AI tools for smarter defense
- Integrate cybersecurity into everyday decisions and leadership conversations

Welcome to **AI in Cybersecurity for SMBs** — let's get secure, smart, and ahead of the curve.

— *Eric LeBouthillier*
Author & Cybersecurity Strategist

For permission requests or inquiries, contact the publisher through the website : www.acrasolution.com

LEGAL DISCLAIMER

Table of Contents

Chapter 1: Understanding AI-Driven Cyber Defense

Introduction

AI is suddenly everywhere — or at least, that's how it feels. Vendors are pitching it, headlines are hyping it, and boardrooms are asking about it. But when it comes to cybersecurity, the term "AI" is often misused, misunderstood, or misapplied — especially in the context of small and mid-sized businesses (SMBs).

For SMB leaders and IT managers, the key question isn't "What is AI?" but rather: **How does it *actually* help protect my business, reduce alert fatigue, or catch attacks that other tools miss?**

That's where the real value lies — and where this chapter focuses.

To cut through the noise, we'll clarify what "AI" really means in cybersecurity (and what it doesn't), how it differs from traditional automation or scripts, the true benefits and risks for SMBs, and why we've reached a critical inflection point where adopting AI-driven defense is no longer optional — it's essential.

What "AI" Really Means in Cybersecurity

If you've ever wondered whether that new "AI-powered" tool is actually intelligent or just automated, you're not alone. Let's break down the key differences.

Defining the Terms Clearly

- **Artificial Intelligence (AI):**
  In cybersecurity, AI typically refers to machine learning systems that *adapt* over time. These systems analyze massive datasets — such as user behavior, file activity, or network traffic — and learn to recognize suspicious patterns that traditional rule sets would miss.
- **Automation:**
  These are predefined rules or workflows that execute without human input. For example, automatically isolating a machine when malware is detected, or sending alerts when a login fails three times in a row.
- **Scripting:**
  Scripting is a form of low-level automation. It uses custom code to perform repetitive tasks — like pulling log data or resetting expired passwords. Unlike AI, scripts don't adapt or improve unless edited by a human.

Key Distinction:
AI *learns from data*. Automation and scripts *follow instructions*. Only AI can spot a never-before-seen attack using predictive modeling.

AI	Automation	Scripting
Uses algorithms to learn and adapt	Performs tasks automatically based on predefined rules	Executes a sequence of predefined commands
Pratctical Cybersecurity Evample Detecting new malware variations	**Practical Cyberscuity Example** Blocking IP addresses on a firewall with preset criteria	**Example** Scanning for vulnerabilities with a custom script

Where AI Is Actually Used in Cyber Defense

In real-world SMB environments, AI is most effective in the following areas:

- **Email Security:**
  Detects phishing attempts using language analysis, sender behavior, and spoofing techniques beyond static filters.
- **Endpoint Protection:**
  Uses behavioral models to detect malware without needing known signatures.
- **User Behavior Analytics (UBA):**
  Builds baselines of normal activity to flag anomalous logins, access patterns, or file movement.
- **SIEM and XDR Platforms:**
  Correlates and prioritizes alerts based on context — not just matching rule sets — to reduce noise and accelerate response.

The Benefits of AI for SMBs

AI levels the playing field. Ten years ago, predictive security analytics were reserved for enterprises with deep pockets. Today, AI-powered tools are built directly into affordable platforms that SMBs already use or can easily adopt.

Top Advantages for SMB Security Leaders

- **Earlier Detection of Advanced Threats:**
  AI catches subtle signals that human analysts or legacy tools may overlook — including zero-day threats and polymorphic malware.
- **Lower Operational Overhead:**
  AI reduces the volume of low-priority alerts, enabling lean IT teams to focus on what truly matters.

- **24/7 Monitoring Without Burnout:**
  AI doesn't sleep. It keeps watch at all hours, detecting lateral movement or insider threats that unfold over days or weeks.
- **Real-Time Decision Support:**
  Instead of just alerting, AI-driven systems often *recommend or automate responses* — speeding up containment and resolution.

Why This Matters for SMBs

You don't need a massive SOC (Security Operations Center) or an in-house data science team to benefit. Many modern EDR, MDR, and email security platforms now include AI features that "just work" in the background — provided they're correctly deployed and tuned.

AI essentially gives SMBs:

- **Faster insights**
- **Better prioritization**
- **Protection that evolves alongside threats**

Misconceptions and Pitfalls to Watch For

Despite the benefits, AI in cybersecurity is not a silver bullet. Knowing what it *can't* do is just as important as knowing what it can.

Top Misconceptions

1. **"AI will run our cybersecurity program."**
   No — AI is a tool, not a strategy. It still requires human oversight, governance, and business context to be effective.

2. **“AI is only for big companies.”**
   Increasingly false. Most modern SMB-focused security vendors include AI-driven features in their core offerings.
3. **“AI eliminates the need for IT expertise.”**
   AI helps reduce the workload but doesn’t remove the need for skilled configuration, interpretation, and response planning.

Practical Pitfalls

- Buying “AI” tools without validating their learning model or outputs
- Assuming AI means *fewer breaches* instead of *faster detection*
- Ignoring user training and policy hygiene in favor of technology alone

Why Now Is the Inflection Point

Over the last two years, the cybersecurity landscape has shifted fundamentally. AI is no longer just part of the *defense* — it's now part of the *attack*.

Threat Actors Are Using AI Too

- **AI-generated phishing emails** are more convincing, better written, and tailored to targets using public data.
- **Malicious AI models** like WormGPT and FraudGPT are available on the dark web, empowering non-technical criminals to craft advanced social engineering campaigns.
- **Automated attack chains** can adapt in real time to evade detection — making static defenses obsolete.

At the Same Time, Defenders Have New Tools

- **AI-native EDR and XDR platforms** can detect indicators of compromise without waiting for threat signatures.
- **Email gateways** now use AI to analyze linguistic patterns, intent, and behavioral signals — not just headers and domains.
- **AI-driven anomaly detection** on networks and cloud platforms flags behaviors that no human could track in real time.

The Bottom Line

This isn't a futuristic trend. It's the new reality of cyber defense. If your business is still relying solely on traditional antivirus, basic firewalls, and user vigilance, you're already behind.

SMBs that don't adapt may not get a second chance.

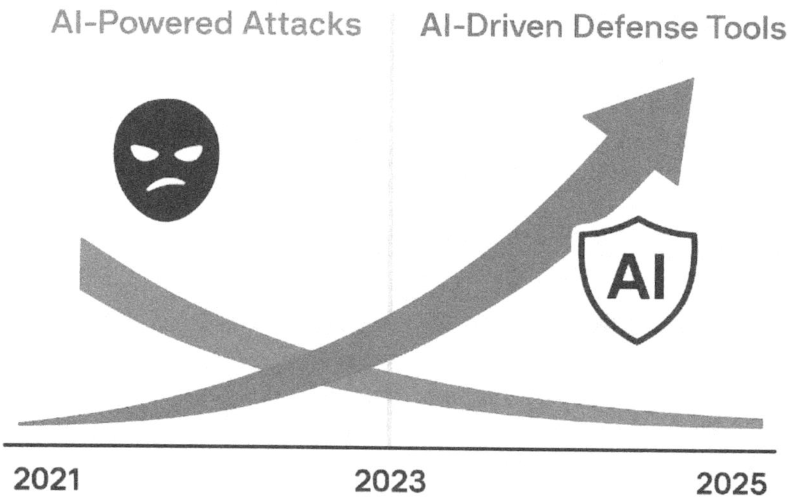

Real-World Example: AI Blocks a CEO Fraud Attempt

What happened:
A regional consulting firm with about 75 employees received an urgent email, seemingly from the CEO, asking the CFO to wire funds to a new vendor. The tone, language, and timing were realistic — it even referenced a recent project discussed in a board meeting.

Why it worked (almost):
The attacker used generative AI to craft the message and pull context from LinkedIn, press releases, and publicly available meeting summaries.

What stopped it:
The firm's AI-enabled email security platform flagged the email based on anomalies in writing style, header metadata, and a behavioral mismatch — the “CEO” had never sent financial requests directly before.

Key takeaway:
Even with flawless grammar and insider language, AI-driven defense detected signals the human eye could not. Without it, this would've been a six-figure loss.

Tactical Best Practices for SMBs

- **Ask vendors for clarity:** What *type* of AI do they use? How is it trained? What data does it analyze?
- **Start with high-impact areas:** Email security and endpoint protection are often the best first steps.
- **Look for contextual alerting:** Good AI tools explain *why* something was flagged — not just that it was.
- **Enable ongoing tuning:** AI improves with feedback. Use tools that let you mark false positives or confirm detections.

Action Checklist

- Audit your current tools — are any AI-enabled or AI-capable?
- Prioritize solutions that apply AI where it matters most (e.g., email, endpoints)
- Involve IT and executive stakeholders in selecting and tuning AI tools
- Train staff to recognize and report suspicious activity — AI is a partner, not a replacement
- Plan a quarterly review of AI system effectiveness and alert quality

---

Conclusion

AI in cybersecurity isn't magic — but it is powerful. For SMBs, the key isn't just buying a tool with "AI" on the label. It's understanding how AI fits into your broader defense strategy, complements your team's capabilities, and keeps pace with modern threats.

By embracing AI where it adds the most value — and avoiding the hype traps — SMBs can gain enterprise-grade defenses at a fraction of the cost, and stay resilient in the face of evolving attacks.

Next Steps

While AI excels at uncovering threats that often slip past human analysts and traditional antivirus tools, detection alone is only half the battle. In the next chapter, we'll explore how AI plays a proactive role in cyber defense — from automated threat response to predictive prevention — helping organizations stay one step ahead of attackers before damage is done.

Chapter 2: How AI Detects Threats Humans Miss

Introduction

Modern cyber threats have outpaced traditional defenses. Attackers no longer rely solely on known malware or brute-force tactics — they exploit subtle weaknesses, live off the land, and maneuver within systems quietly. Small and mid-sized businesses (SMBs) are especially vulnerable, often lacking the resources or staff to keep pace. This is where artificial intelligence (AI) is proving indispensable.

AI-powered cybersecurity isn't just faster — it's fundamentally different. It excels at recognizing the abnormal, the unexpected, and the invisible-to-human patterns that signal a breach. For SMB leaders, understanding how AI detects threats that slip past even seasoned analysts is key to building a future-ready defense.

Behavioral Analytics: Seeing the Story Behind the Activity

Most traditional security tools focus on signatures — predefined rules or known attack patterns. AI changes the game by focusing on **behavior**.

Behavioral analytics monitors how users, systems, and applications typically operate. When something deviates — like a finance manager logging in at 3 a.m. from a new device and downloading gigabytes of data — AI doesn't need a virus signature to sound the alarm.

How It Works

- AI systems ingest massive volumes of baseline data from your network
- They create behavioral profiles for users, endpoints, and apps
- Deviations are flagged, scored, and prioritized for review

These insights enable AI-driven tools to detect threats like:

- Compromised credentials
- Rogue internal activity
- Early stages of ransomware before payload deployment

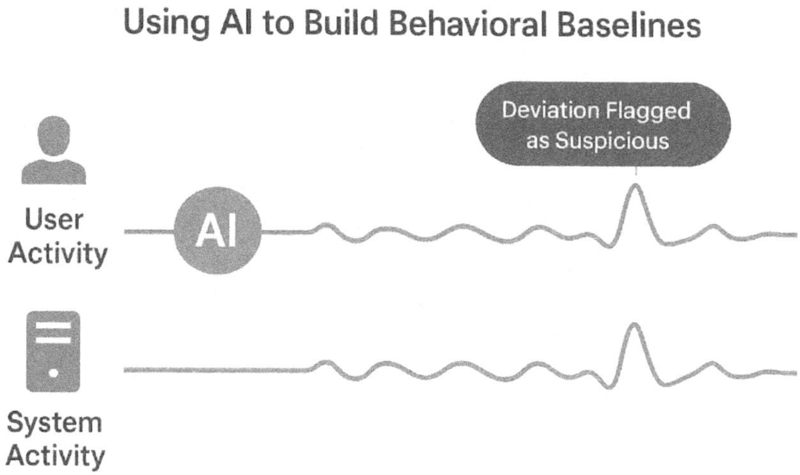

Anomaly Detection and Threat Hunting

AI is particularly skilled at **anomaly detection** — spotting events that don't fit the norm, even if they're not explicitly malicious yet.

Unlike rule-based systems that wait for defined indicators, AI can:

- Identify rare process behavior (e.g., PowerShell executing from a Word doc)
- Detect irregular login patterns across time zones
- Monitor resource use that hints at crypto mining or lateral movement

In more advanced deployments, AI supports **autonomous threat hunting**:

- Continuously scans telemetry data for signs of emerging threats
- Correlates weak signals across disparate systems
- Surfaces stealthy attacks early — without waiting for a breach

Tactical Best Practices

- Prioritize AI tools that support real-time threat scoring
- Ensure your AI solution integrates with existing SIEM or XDR platforms
- Review flagged anomalies regularly to train your team on behavioral indicators

---

Defending Against Fileless Malware and Privilege Abuse

Modern attacks don't always drop files. **Fileless malware** operates in memory, often using legitimate tools like PowerShell or WMI. These threats bypass traditional antivirus (AV) by blending into normal activity.

AI's strength lies in its ability to:

- Spot unusual use of native system tools
- Detect abuse of admin privileges or lateral movement
- Recognize new behavior patterns linked to command-and-control channels

Why Traditional AV Falls Short

Most AV tools need a file, a hash, or a known behavior. Fileless attacks bypass all three. AI doesn't rely on static signatures — it assesses **intent and behavior** in real time.

Common Pitfalls to Avoid

- Relying solely on legacy AV to stop advanced persistent threats
- Ignoring alerts on legitimate tools being used suspiciously
- Failing to monitor privilege escalation or internal movement

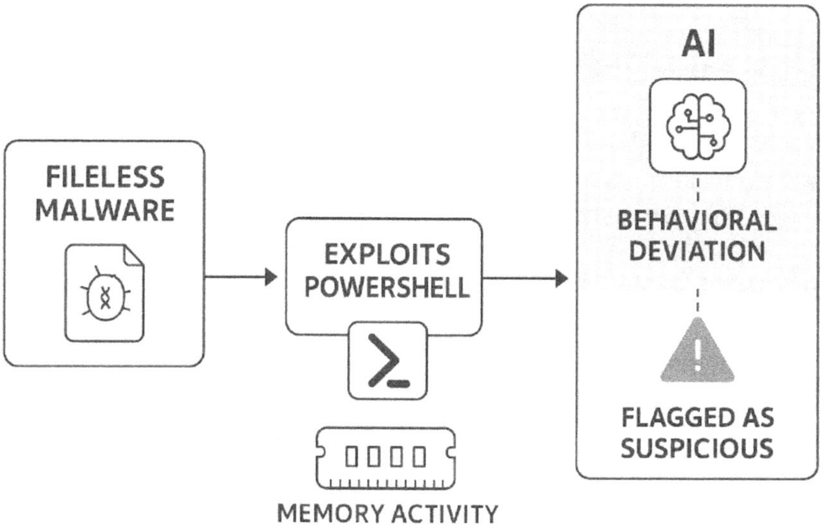

Real-World Comparison: AI vs. Traditional Antivirus

Let's look at a real scenario from a mid-sized accounting firm:

What Happened

An attacker gained access through a stolen VPN credential. There was no malware file — only a series of remote PowerShell commands used to explore the network and escalate privileges. The firm's traditional AV showed no alerts.

Meanwhile, their AI-based endpoint detection system flagged:

- Unusual PowerShell usage from a finance workstation
- Anomalous account activity during off-hours
- Access to servers the user had never touched before

A junior analyst received a prioritized alert and shut down the session within minutes — stopping data exfiltration before it began.

What Went Right

- Behavioral analytics caught what signatures missed
- Autonomous anomaly detection reduced response time
- AI helped a small IT team act decisively

What We Learn

- AI levels the playing field for SMBs
- Even unsophisticated attacks are detectable through behavior
- A fast, automated response beats signature-based detection every time

Why This Matters for SMB Security

SMBs often assume advanced tools are out of reach — but AI is increasingly baked into modern cybersecurity platforms. From endpoint detection to cloud monitoring, vendors now offer AI-enhanced solutions tailored for smaller teams and limited budgets.

Checklist: What to Look For in AI-Driven Detection

- Behavioral baselining and continuous anomaly detection
- Visibility into fileless attacks and internal threats
- Integration with your existing network and endpoint tools
- Human-friendly dashboards with explainable alerts

Traditional AV	AI Detection
Intrusion Signature-based scanning	Analyzes anomalties in behavior
Execution Known file-based threats	Detects fileless attacks
Persistence Relies on regular updates	Adaptable in real time
Lateral Movement Limited detection capabili-	Identifies suspicious activity

Conclusion

AI isn't just a buzzword — it's a force multiplier. By focusing on behaviors instead of signatures, it enables SMBs to catch the kinds of threats that evade traditional defenses. Whether it's stopping fileless malware, catching compromised users, or accelerating threat response, AI allows smaller teams to punch above their weight.

In today's threat landscape, standing still is falling behind. Adopting AI-driven detection means staying proactive, agile, and resilient — even without a massive security team.

Next Steps

Start by evaluating your current endpoint and network security stack. Look for AI-native platforms or modules that add behavioral analytics and anomaly detection. Focus on explainability — AI alerts should make sense to your team, not mystify them.

In the next chapter, we'll look at a high-risk attack vector most SMBs face daily: email. We'll explore how AI is transforming real-time scanning to detect phishing, impersonation, and even deepfake attachments — before they reach your users.

Chapter 3: Real-Time Email Scanning with AI

Introduction

Email remains the single most exploited entry point for cyberattacks. For SMBs, one click from a distracted employee can unleash ransomware, expose sensitive data, or trigger costly fraud. Traditional spam filters and antivirus scanners are no longer enough. Today's email threats are adaptive, fast-moving, and engineered to evade conventional defenses.

Artificial Intelligence (AI) is transforming how we protect the inbox. By analyzing the context, intent, and subtle signals behind every message, AI can detect threats that legacy systems miss — including sophisticated phishing, deepfake attachments, and impersonation attempts. For resource-constrained SMBs, AI-enabled email protection offers a practical and powerful layer of defense.

Understanding the Modern Email Threat Landscape

Email attacks have evolved far beyond obvious spam or virus-laden attachments. Threat actors now use:

- Social engineering and emotional manipulation
- Business email compromise (BEC) tactics
- Fileless payloads hidden in cloud links or macros
- AI-generated content that mimics real communication

Traditional email security systems depend on blacklists, signatures, and known threats. Unfortunately, modern phishing kits rotate domains, mimic trusted brands, and often create unique messages for each recipient — making them virtually undetectable by static rules.

Common Threat Types AI Helps Detect

- CEO impersonation and supplier fraud
- Invoice manipulation or payment redirection
- Credential harvesting via lookalike login pages
- Deepfake audio/video attachments used for deception

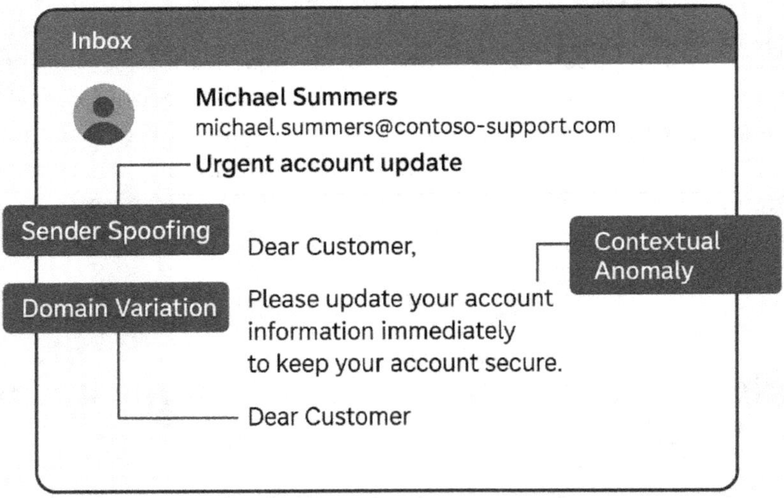

How AI Understands Email Beyond Keywords

AI doesn't just scan email content for bad words or links. It applies Natural Language Processing (NLP) to interpret **intent, tone, and structure** — allowing it to uncover hidden risks even in clean-looking messages.

Key Capabilities of NLP-Powered Email AI

- **Semantic Analysis**: Understands meaning, not just phrasing (e.g., "Can you process this wire urgently?")
- **Sender Behavior Profiling**: Flags emails from familiar domains with unfamiliar behavior
- **Contextual Anomaly Detection**: Recognizes when a request is unusual for the sender or recipient
- **Attachment and Link Analysis**: Inspects embedded links and documents in real time, even if hosted in cloud services

This allows AI to detect:

- Slight deviations in grammar or structure from known contacts
- Unusual requests or urgent tone that suggest social engineering
- Synthetic or generated language common in mass phishing

Tactical Best Practices

- Choose email security solutions that analyze content **and** behavior
- Enable AI-based scanning on both inbound and internal communications
- Use systems that explain why a message was flagged — transparency builds trust

Deepfakes, Impersonation, and Identity Abuse

As generative AI tools become more accessible, attackers can now craft near-perfect impersonations. From fake voice clips of a CEO requesting wire transfers to deepfake videos embedded in attachments, the bar for deception has been raised.

AI can help detect these next-gen threats by:

- Comparing voice or writing style against known baselines
- Identifying inconsistencies in metadata or message flow
- Flagging sudden shifts in behavior (e.g., CFO sending a video from a new device in a different country)

Even internally, identity spoofing can cause damage. A threat actor inside your environment might send a believable phishing email from a compromised account. AI's ability to evaluate context and behavioral patterns adds a critical layer of defense.

Checklist: How AI Spots Impersonation

- Unusual time-of-day activity from trusted accounts
- Changes in email signature or tone
- Anomalous IP or device fingerprint for the sender
- Requests for atypical actions or financial transactions

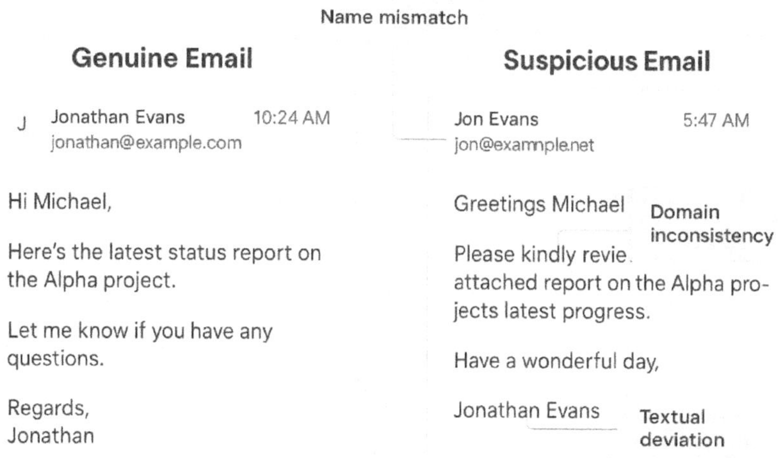

Real-World Example: AI Thwarts Executive Impersonation Scam

What Happened

A regional logistics company received an urgent email from what appeared to be the CFO, requesting a same-day wire transfer to a new vendor. The message was brief, used the correct email address format, and even included the CFO's typical sign-off. The accounting team was prepared to act — until their AI-powered email filter flagged it for "sender behavior anomaly."

Upon investigation, it was revealed that:

- The domain was a subtle variation (one letter off)
- The tone of the email was unusually terse
- The vendor had never been referenced in prior communication
- The sending IP originated from a foreign country

What Went Right

- AI flagged the email before it reached the user
- Alert included clear rationale: domain mismatch, unusual tone, and suspicious sender behavior
- IT followed up, preventing a $25,000 fraud attempt

What We Learn

- Even highly convincing impersonations can be defeated by AI trained on normal communication patterns
- NLP and context-aware scanning are far more effective than static filters
- Fast, understandable alerts help teams act with confidence

Tools That Use AI for Email Protection

Today's market offers several AI-powered tools designed specifically for SMBs. These platforms integrate seamlessly with existing email infrastructure (Microsoft 365, Google Workspace) and enhance protection without requiring large security teams.

Leading AI Email Security Platforms

- **Darktrace/Email**: Uses behavioral AI to monitor communication flow and flag anomalies
- **Area 1 Security** (now part of Cloudflare): Focuses on pre-delivery protection using NLP and link analysis
- **Abnormal Security**: Profiles normal behavior across your org to detect phishing, BEC, and internal threats
- **Mimecast and Proofpoint AI Modules**: Add advanced AI detection to traditional secure email gateways

What to Look For

- Compatibility with your current email platform
- Behavioral baselining of internal and external communications
- Transparent scoring and alert explanations
- Auto-remediation (e.g., pulling malicious emails post-delivery)

AI Email Security Tools

	Detection Features	SMB-Friendliness	Ease of Deployment
Defender for Office 365	Phishing Detection	✓	✓
Armorblox	Phishing	✓	✓
Avanan	BEC Protection	✓	✓
Vade	Attachment Analysis	✓	✓
		✓	✓

Conclusion

Email remains a high-risk attack vector, but AI is dramatically improving how we defend it. By analyzing message intent, user behavior, and subtle anomalies, AI can detect threats that humans — and legacy filters — routinely miss. For SMBs, this means greater security with less overhead.

No solution is perfect, but an AI-augmented approach gives your business a critical edge. With the right tools in place, you can drastically reduce your risk from phishing, fraud, and impersonation — without slowing down productivity.

Next Steps

Evaluate your current email protection layers. Do they go beyond spam filtering? Look for AI-based platforms that offer behavior analysis, deep NLP, and impersonation defense. Ensure your team understands the alerts and knows how to act on them.

In the next chapter, we'll zoom in on another critical AI application: endpoint defense. We'll explore how next-gen antivirus and EDR platforms use AI to stop zero-day exploits, insider threats, and ransomware before damage is done.

Chapter 4: AI for Endpoint Defense

Introduction

Cybercriminals don't need to breach your data center — they just need to compromise one laptop, server, or mobile device. Endpoints are where work gets done and where attacks most often begin. And while traditional antivirus (AV) tools were once sufficient, today's threats move too fast and adapt too cleverly for static defenses to keep up.

That's where Artificial Intelligence (AI) enters the picture. AI is the engine behind next-generation antivirus and endpoint detection and response (EDR) platforms. It doesn't just scan files — it understands behavior, monitors activity in real time, and responds at machine speed. For SMBs, AI-powered endpoint defense means gaining enterprise-grade protection without enterprise complexity.

The Evolution of Endpoint Security

Legacy antivirus tools rely on known signatures — digital fingerprints of previously discovered malware. They're effective against old threats, but fall short against:

- Zero-day exploits
- Fileless attacks
- Living-off-the-land tactics (using legitimate tools for malicious purposes)

AI-based systems take a fundamentally different approach:

- They **learn baseline behavior** for applications, users, and processes
- They **identify anomalies** that signal malicious activity
- They **respond autonomously** — blocking processes, isolating devices, or alerting security teams

This shift from reactive to **proactive, behavior-based defense** is what defines next-gen endpoint security.

Tactical Best Practices

- Replace or augment traditional AV with an AI-based EDR platform
- Use solutions with real-time behavior analysis and automated containment
- Prioritize tools that work across Windows, macOS, and mobile endpoints

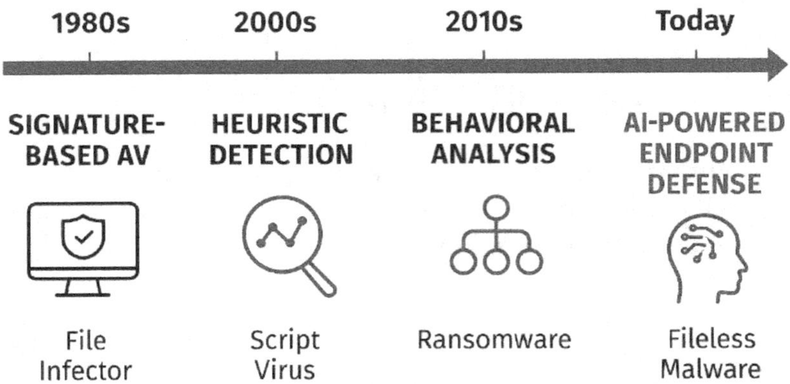

EVOLUTION From Alsmal ENDPOINT DDEFENSE

Stopping Zero-Day Threats and Insider Abuse

Zero-day threats exploit unknown vulnerabilities. By definition, there are no signatures to detect them. AI steps in by spotting unusual behavior — not just known indicators.

AI excels at detecting:

- Sudden changes in process behavior (e.g., a web browser spawning PowerShell)
- Unusual privilege escalation attempts
- New executable files behaving suspiciously on endpoints

Similarly, **insider threats** — whether malicious or accidental — are notoriously hard to detect. Traditional tools assume users are trustworthy. AI doesn't.

It watches for:

- Access to files or systems outside of a user's normal pattern
- Data exfiltration attempts via USB or cloud sharing tools
- Rapid or bulk file deletions or modifications

Common Pitfalls to Avoid

- Relying on signature-only AV to catch advanced threats
- Ignoring the behavior of privileged users
- Delaying updates to EDR software due to perceived complexity

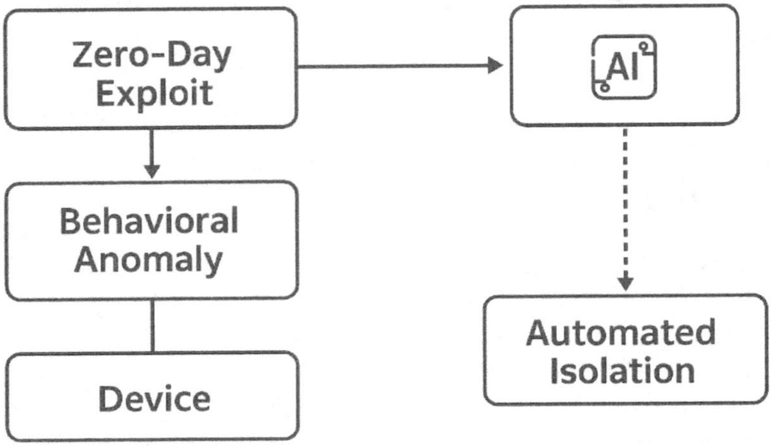

AI detecting a Zero-Day Exploit via Behavioral Anomaly

Real-World Case Study: AI Stops Lateral Movement in a Mid-Sized Business

What Happened

An attacker gained access to an SMB's network via a compromised endpoint — a marketing employee's laptop with a weak password. Instead of dropping ransomware immediately, the attacker used legitimate Windows tools to move laterally and search for high-value targets.

Fortunately, the company had deployed an AI-based EDR platform that:

- Flagged the unusual use of PsExec (a tool rarely used outside IT)
- Detected unauthorized access attempts to a file server
- Automatically quarantined the compromised endpoint within 90 seconds

The incident was contained before data could be exfiltrated or encrypted.

What Went Right

- AI recognized behavioral anomalies in real time
- Response was automated — no need to wait for human review
- The IT team received clear, actionable insights for forensics and recovery

What We Learn

- Even well-camouflaged attacks can be caught by behavioral AI
- Autonomous response capabilities drastically shorten dwell time
- SMBs can defend against advanced tactics without dedicated SOC teams

---

AI-Driven Features That Matter for SMBs

When evaluating AI-powered endpoint solutions, focus on features that deliver real protection with minimal overhead.

Checklist: What to Look for in an AI-Based Endpoint Platform

- **Behavioral threat detection**: Identifies abnormal application or user activity
- **Automated response**: Isolates endpoints, blocks processes, and rolls back changes
- **Cloud-native management**: Enables visibility and control from anywhere
- **Lightweight agent design**: Won't slow down user machines
- **Built-in threat intelligence**: Correlates local events with global threat trends

Top SMB-Friendly Platforms Using AI

- **SentinelOne**: Fully autonomous EDR with rollback and threat hunting capabilities
- **CrowdStrike Falcon**: Cloud-delivered AI that stops malware and fileless threats
- **Microsoft Defender for Business**: Built-in for many Microsoft 365 users, increasingly AI-driven
- **Sophos Intercept X**: Uses deep learning to block zero-days and includes anti-ransomware features

	Platform A	Platform B	Platform D
Feature Comparrasiny ꟻ AI-Enpoint Security Platformas Platforms			
Detection	Behavioral Analysis Threat Intelligence Integration	Benavioral Analysis Threat Intelligence Integration	Behavioral Analysis Threat Intelligence Integration
Response Automated Remediation	✓ Automated Remediation	✓ Automated Remediation	✓ Incident Investigation
Usability Intuitive Interlace Lightweight Agent	✓ Intuitive Interface Lightweight Agent	✓ Intuitive Interface Lightweight Agent	✓ Lightweight Agent Flexible Licensing
Cost-Efficiency	✓ Competitive Pricing	✓ Flexible Licensing	✓ Flexible Licensing

Conclusion

AI-powered endpoint defense represents a seismic shift in how small and mid-sized businesses can protect themselves. Instead of waiting for known malware to strike, these systems monitor behavior, detect early indicators of compromise, and act autonomously — all while providing your team with clear, explainable insights.

For SMBs operating with lean IT staff, AI delivers the vigilance and speed of a much larger security operation. It helps prevent not just external breaches, but internal misuse and human error — making it a smart investment in resilience.

Next Steps

Assess your current endpoint protection. Is it behavior-based? Does it offer automated response or rollback? Look at AI-capable platforms that provide visibility across all devices — and ideally integrate with your broader security ecosystem.

In the next chapter, we'll explore how AI is reshaping identity protection — helping detect unusual login behavior, defend against account takeover, and simplify secure access for your users.

Chapter 5: Leveraging AI for Login & Identity Monitoring

Introduction

Your cybersecurity is only as strong as your ability to control who gets in — and how. Every successful data breach, ransomware attack, or account hijack starts with one thing: compromised credentials. For SMBs, managing identity has become a balancing act between security and usability. You need protection that's intelligent — not intrusive.

That's where AI changes the game. By analyzing login behavior, device patterns, and access history in real time, AI can detect when a login attempt doesn't fit the norm — even if the username and password are technically correct. When paired with smart multi-factor authentication (MFA) and adaptive access controls, AI helps keep accounts secure without frustrating legitimate users.

Why Identity Is the New Security Perimeter

In today's cloud-first world, employees access data from anywhere — across devices, apps, and networks. Firewalls and VPNs no longer define your perimeter. **Identity now is your first and most critical line of defense.**

Unfortunately, most SMBs rely on basic tools:

- Static usernames and passwords
- Traditional MFA that's the same for every login
- Reactive alerts that come too late

Attackers exploit these limitations through:

- Credential stuffing
- Phishing and social engineering
- Session hijacking or token theft

AI brings proactive defense by:

- Building behavior profiles per user
- Scanning for anomalous login attempts in real time
- Triggering step-up authentication or blocking high-risk access automatically

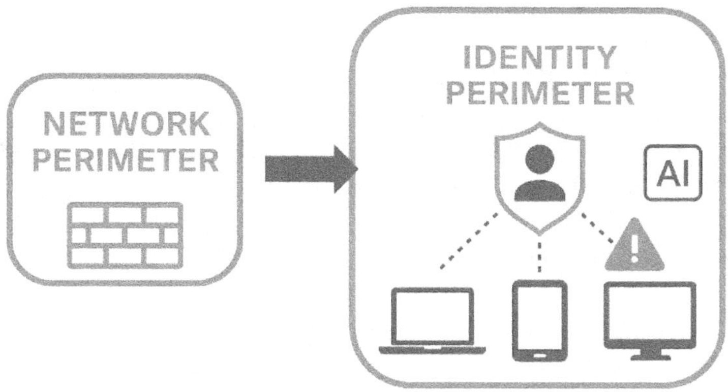

Abnormal login behavior

Detecting Unusual Login Behavior

Traditional access logs are noisy and difficult to interpret. AI cuts through the clutter by continuously learning what "normal" looks like for each user:

- Typical login times
- Common devices and browsers
- Usual geolocations
- Accessed apps and services

When something deviates — say, a 2 a.m. login from a new device in a different country — AI raises the alarm. Better yet, it can take immediate action.

How AI Detects Risky Logins

- **Impossible Travel**: Detects logins from geographically distant locations in too short a time span
- **First-Time Access**: Flags first-time access to sensitive apps or data
- **Session Hijack Detection**: Monitors for token misuse or unusual session lengths
- **Device Fingerprinting**: Identifies logins from unrecognized hardware or virtual machines

Tactical Best Practices

- Use identity providers or platforms with AI-based risk scoring (e.g., Microsoft Entra ID, Okta, Duo)
- Review high-risk login reports weekly
- Link login monitoring to automatic access control rules (e.g., deny access from unmanaged devices)

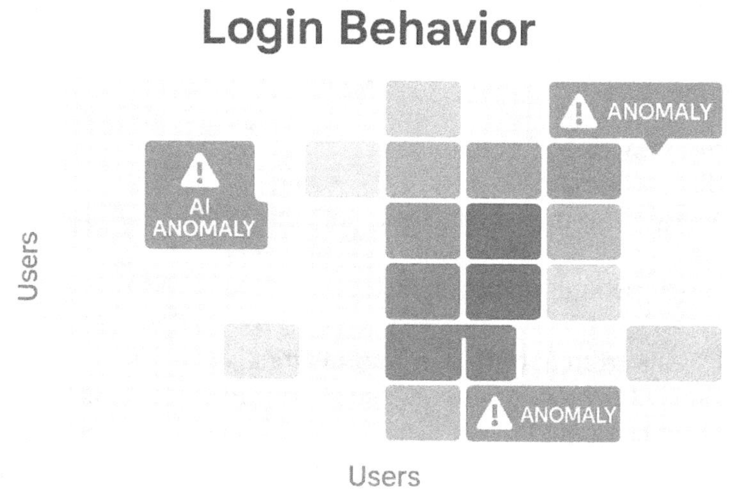

MFA Intelligence and Account Takeover Defense

Multi-factor authentication (MFA) is a must — but AI makes it smarter. Instead of requiring the same MFA challenge every time, AI can adapt based on context:

- Known device? Skip MFA.
- New country + high-value app? Step up to stronger verification.

AI-enhanced MFA systems assess **risk in real time** and apply controls accordingly.

Account Takeover (ATO) Detection with AI

Even with MFA, attackers still succeed through:

- Stolen sessions or cookies
- SIM-swapping
- Man-in-the-middle phishing kits that relay MFA codes

AI catches these attempts by spotting:

- Logins from automation frameworks
- Reused behavior patterns across multiple accounts (bot-like login behavior)
- Sessions behaving differently than typical user sessions (e.g., rapid navigation to payment systems)

Checklist: Smart MFA with AI Should Offer

- Adaptive challenges based on login risk
- Biometric or phishing-resistant options (e.g., FIDO2, push-based authentication)
- Visibility into bypass attempts or MFA fatigue attacks (e.g., repeated push prompts)

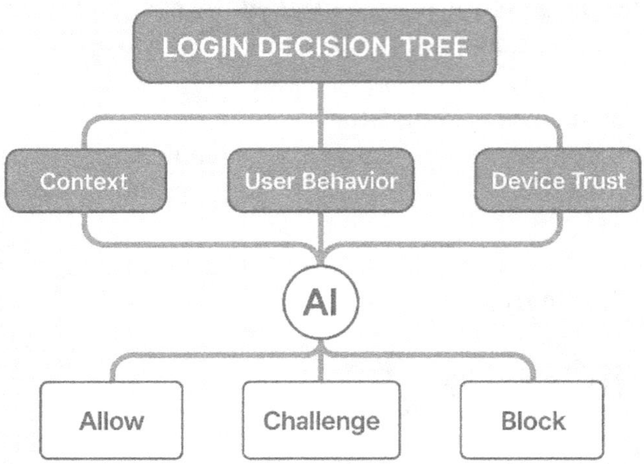

Real-World Use Case: Simplified Secure Logins at a Growing SMB

What Happened

A 50-person marketing firm wanted to improve account security without increasing helpdesk tickets or frustrating users. They were using basic email-password combos and occasional MFA via SMS — which wasn't scalable.

They implemented a cloud-based identity provider with built-in AI monitoring and adaptive MFA. Over the next 60 days:

- Users received fewer MFA prompts when logging in from trusted devices
- High-risk logins (e.g., new devices from abroad) triggered push-based MFA or were blocked
- A compromised account was detected within minutes when a login came from a Tor browser — something that user had never done before

What Went Right

- AI detected account compromise before damage occurred
- Smart MFA reduced friction while increasing protection
- Admins had full visibility into login risk across all apps

What We Learn

- AI helps balance security with usability — critical for growing SMBs
- Risk-based access control reduces friction without weakening defenses
- Fast detection and automated policy enforcement prevent escalation

SMB-Friendly Platforms That Offer AI Identity Protection

You don't need to be an enterprise to benefit from AI-enhanced identity tools. Many cloud platforms now bake intelligent monitoring into their offerings.

Leading Tools with AI-Powered Login Monitoring

- **Microsoft Entra ID (formerly Azure AD)**: Built-in risk-based conditional access for Microsoft 365 users
- **Okta Behavior Detection**: Monitors user behavior and integrates with third-party apps
- **Duo Beyond (Cisco)**: AI-driven access control with contextual MFA
- **JumpCloud**: Identity and device trust unified with behavior-aware policies
- **Google Workspace Admin Console**: Includes suspicious login detection and session insights

Common Pitfalls to Avoid

- Treating MFA as a checkbox rather than a dynamic control
- Ignoring login data from mobile and third-party apps
- Relying solely on end-user reporting of suspicious access

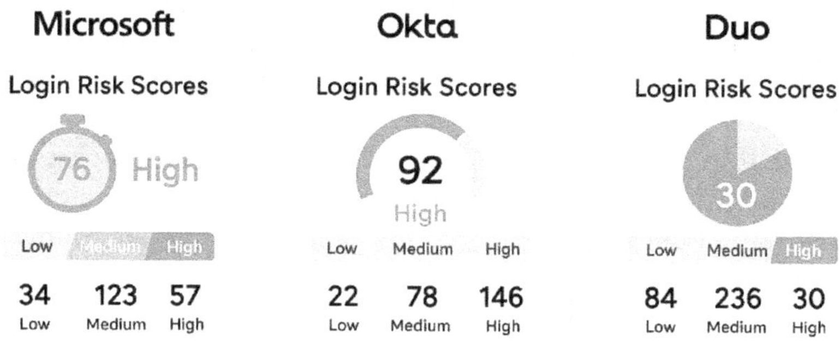

Conclusion

Login credentials are the most targeted asset in your business — and AI gives you a powerful edge in defending them. By monitoring behavior in real time, adapting access requirements based on context, and flagging anomalies that humans miss, AI transforms identity security from a compliance task into a strategic advantage.

For SMBs, this means you can achieve secure, scalable logins that your users won't hate — and that attackers won't easily bypass.

Next Steps

Review your identity provider or SSO setup. Does it offer behavioral analytics or contextual MFA? If not, consider upgrading to a solution that does. Start with your highest-risk user groups (finance, executives, remote workers) and roll out adaptive policies gradually.

Next, we'll explore how AI continues working behind the scenes in your **cloud and SaaS environments** — identifying suspicious usage, fixing risky misconfigurations, and delivering alerts that SMB teams can actually use.

Chapter 6: How AI Monitors Cloud & SaaS Behavior

Introduction

As SMBs move more of their operations into cloud platforms like Microsoft 365, Google Workspace, and Dropbox, their risk surface expands dramatically. The same convenience that enables anywhere-access also introduces new blind spots — data shared too broadly, misconfigured permissions, or users engaging with apps that bypass IT entirely.

Traditional monitoring tools weren't built for this environment. Logs are fragmented, and threats often appear as subtle behavior shifts, not signature-based events. That's where AI becomes indispensable. By continuously analyzing usage patterns across cloud apps and SaaS platforms, AI can detect suspicious activity, flag risky exposure, and help SMBs take action — even without a large IT team.

The Challenge: Visibility in the Cloud

In the traditional on-prem world, IT had full control over user access and network traffic. In the cloud? Not so much.

Employees now:

- Share files with outside parties in seconds
- Connect third-party apps with a single OAuth click
- Log in from personal devices, unmanaged networks, or even other countries

Meanwhile, sensitive data — client contracts, financial records, intellectual property — lives in Google Drive, OneDrive, SharePoint, or Dropbox folders that may be shared far beyond what's intended.

AI bridges the gap by:

- Analyzing usage and sharing behaviors continuously
- Detecting when access patterns don't fit established norms
- Surfacing actionable alerts instead of overwhelming logs

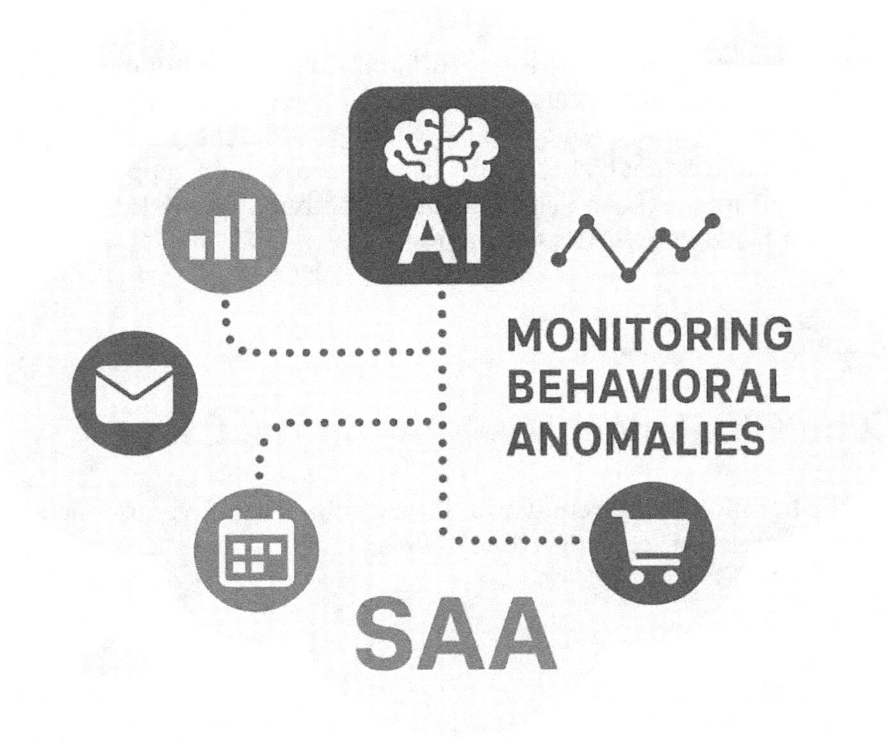

Detecting Suspicious Usage in SaaS Platforms

Every SaaS app has its own logging and alerting system — if it has one at all. AI-powered cloud security platforms unify this chaos, creating a centralized behavioral profile for users and apps across the board.

What AI Looks For

- **Unusual File Access**: A user suddenly downloads large volumes of data or accesses documents they've never touched before
- **Login Pattern Deviations**: Access to cloud storage from new countries, devices, or networks
- **Shadow IT Detection**: Identifies users connecting unsanctioned apps or tools
- **Unusual Sharing Behavior**: Sensitive documents shared externally or via public links

Tactical Best Practices

- Use a Cloud Access Security Broker (CASB) or SaaS security tool that includes AI monitoring
- Enable integration across all major platforms — Google Workspace, Microsoft 365, Dropbox, Slack, etc.
- Set policy thresholds for download limits, external sharing, and unusual login geographies

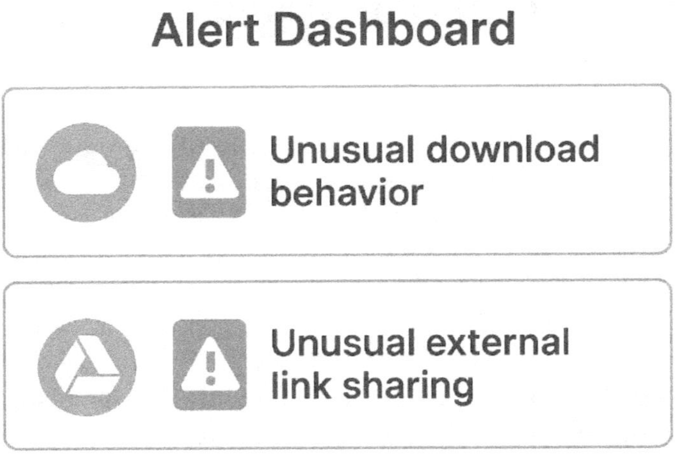

Fixing Misconfigurations and Over-Shared Files

Misconfigurations — not malware — are among the top causes of cloud data exposure. AI systems can detect when your data is at risk **before** it's exploited.

Common Cloud Risks AI Can Catch

- Folders with **"Anyone with the link"** access that contain sensitive content
- Publicly shared calendars exposing internal meeting links
- Admin accounts with **no MFA enabled**
- Users granted **broad access** when they only need narrow permissions

AI tools not only identify these risks — they often recommend and even automate remediation:

- Revoking outdated shares
- Enforcing stricter sharing policies
- Flagging inactive users with lingering access

Common Pitfalls to Avoid

- Assuming built-in cloud platform alerts are enough
- Failing to audit third-party app integrations regularly
- Ignoring over-permissioned accounts (especially dormant ones)

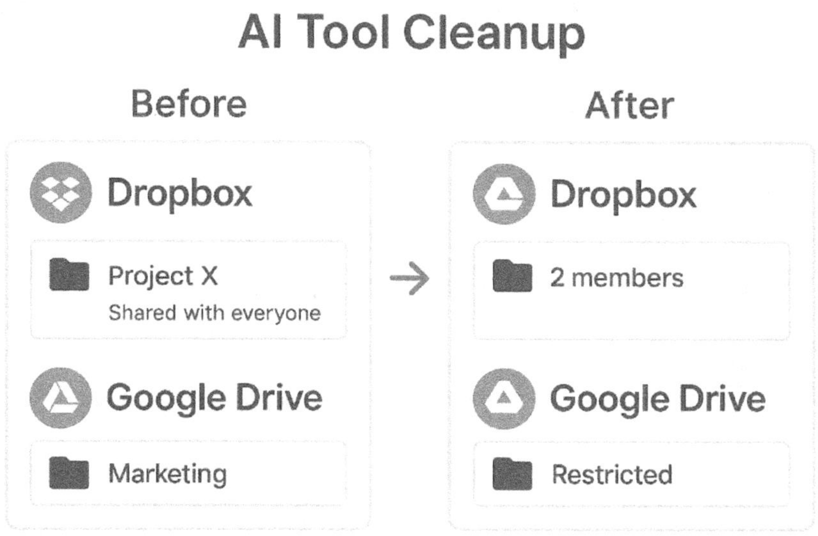

Real-World Example: Preventing Data Leakage in a Remote SMB

What Happened

A 30-person architecture firm had transitioned fully to Google Workspace during the pandemic. As the team grew and onboarded new contractors, sharing controls loosened — with little oversight.

Their AI-enhanced SaaS security tool flagged:

- Sensitive design files shared with personal Gmail accounts
- A contractor downloading 600+ files in 24 hours
- An app integration that requested full Drive access without IT approval

The system auto-revoked risky shares, notified the admin, and recommended removing the unused app.

What Went Right

- AI flagged suspicious patterns that weren't malicious — just risky
- Alerts were clear, relevant, and actionable
- No data was lost or leaked, and employee access was not interrupted

What We Learn

- SMBs face real exposure risks from normal operations
- AI helps strike the right balance between access and control
- Quick intervention prevents future incidents

Alerts That SMBs Can Actually Act On

One of the biggest frustrations for SMBs is alert fatigue. Many platforms either bombard teams with irrelevant warnings — or provide zero context. AI helps solve this by:

- Prioritizing alerts based on severity and context
- Explaining **why** something is risky
- Suggesting or even implementing fixes

What Makes an AI Alert Useful?

- **Specific**: Tells you which file, user, or app is involved
- **Contextual**: Shows how behavior differs from the norm
- **Actionable**: Offers clear steps or auto-remediation options
- **Non-disruptive**: Avoids unnecessary blocks or interruptions

Checklist: Alert Policies That Work for SMBs

- Flag external shares of files with financial, legal, or HR keywords
- Detect and log third-party app OAuth approvals
- Alert on unusual download or sharing spikes per user
- Notify admins of any logins from new countries or TOR networks

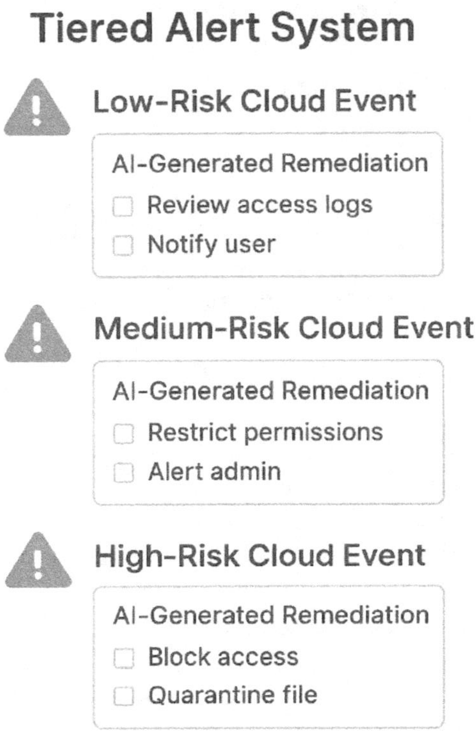

Conclusion

As your business increasingly relies on cloud and SaaS tools, your most valuable data is often one misconfiguration or careless click away from exposure. AI transforms cloud security from passive monitoring into proactive risk reduction — automatically detecting, prioritizing, and mitigating risky behavior across your environment.

For SMBs, this means fewer breaches, better compliance, and more time spent growing your business instead of chasing down vague warnings or fixing self-inflicted leaks.

Next Steps

Audit your current cloud environment. Are you getting meaningful visibility into file sharing, app usage, and login behavior? Look for AI-powered tools that unify monitoring across platforms and offer smart, automated alerts. The best solutions don't just detect problems — they help you fix them.

Next, we'll shift focus to a risk that's outside your walls — your vendors. In **Chapter 7**, we'll show how AI can help assess third-party risk, flag compromised partners, and protect your business from supply chain breaches.

Chapter 7: When AI Flags Vendor or Supply Chain Risk

Introduction

Your cybersecurity isn't just about your own defenses — it's about everyone you're connected to. Whether it's a cloud service provider, a billing software vendor, or a third-party IT consultant, your business relies on an extended digital supply chain. And every link in that chain is a potential attack vector.

Recent breaches — from SolarWinds to Okta integrations — have proven that even trusted partners can become conduits for compromise. For SMBs, the challenge is knowing **which vendors** pose risk and **when** to take action. That's where AI comes in. By analyzing reputation signals, breach history, and behavioral anomalies across your vendor landscape, AI can flag threats that humans would miss — before damage occurs.

Why Supply Chain Risk Is Rising for SMBs

Today, every SMB operates in a connected ecosystem:

- Cloud-hosted apps
- Outsourced IT services
- External software dependencies
- API-integrated vendors

This web of connections brings efficiency — but also exposes your business to:

- Breaches through trusted partner credentials
- Malware or backdoors delivered through legitimate software updates
- Compliance failures triggered by insecure third-party data handling

Most SMBs lack dedicated vendor risk management teams, which means risks often go unnoticed until it's too late.

AI changes the equation by:

- Continuously evaluating vendor behavior and reputation
- Correlating breach history and threat intelligence data
- Surfacing actionable insights, not endless spreadsheets

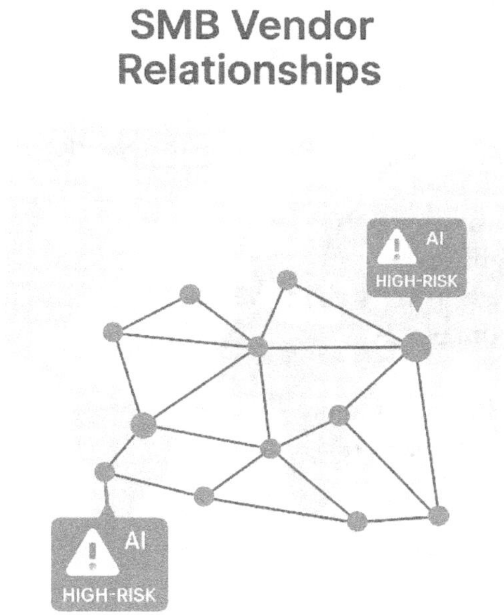

Reputation Scoring and Breach Correlation

Not all vendors are created equal. Some have strong security controls, transparent policies, and a clean breach history. Others may be poorly maintained or already compromised — but you'd never know unless you had hours to research every one.

AI tools can now assign **dynamic reputation scores** based on:

- Public breach records and CVEs (Common Vulnerabilities and Exposures)
- Third-party risk feeds and dark web chatter
- SSL certificate hygiene, DNS records, and misconfiguration scans
- Historical software patching behavior

What a Reputation Score Tells You

- **Recent breach exposure** (was this vendor involved in a known incident?)
- **Risky software behavior** (do their updates or apps include vulnerabilities?)
- **Security maturity** (how well do they manage authentication, encryption, etc.?)

This empowers SMBs to make smarter choices — not just based on price or features, but actual risk posture.

Checklist: Using AI for Reputation Monitoring

- Set up continuous scoring for all vendors with data or system access
- Prioritize review of vendors flagged as "high-risk" after changes in score
- Map vendor scores to your data sensitivity — more sensitive = stricter thresholds

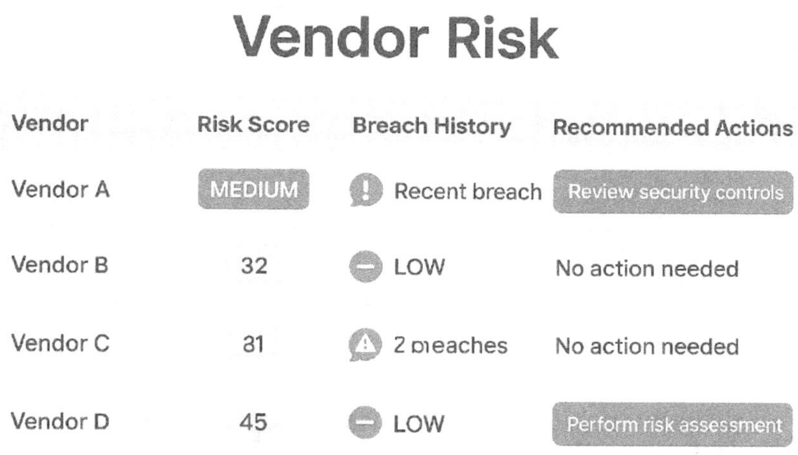

Vendor Risk

Vendor	Risk Score	Breach History	Recommended Actions
Vendor A	MEDIUM	Recent breach	Review security controls
Vendor B	32	LOW	No action needed
Vendor C	31	2 breaches	No action needed
Vendor D	45	LOW	Perform risk assessment

Risk Signals Across Updates, APIs, and Cloud Vendors

A compromised vendor update can be more dangerous than malware — because it looks legitimate. Supply chain attacks often enter through:

- Software patches or updates containing hidden backdoors
- OAuth connections or API tokens reused across multiple platforms

- Admin access granted to third-party tools without full visibility

AI systems can detect:

- Sudden changes in software behavior after an update
- New, unusual data flows between your systems and vendor platforms
- Excessive permission requests from vendor-connected applications

Tactical Best Practices

- Use endpoint and network monitoring tools with AI to flag post-update behavior
- Review vendor integrations and OAuth scopes regularly
- Combine cloud access logs with third-party risk intelligence for full context

Common Pitfalls

- Blindly trusting software updates from small vendors
- Allowing vendors to retain privileged access long after onboarding
- Using unmanaged integrations with no logging or audit trail

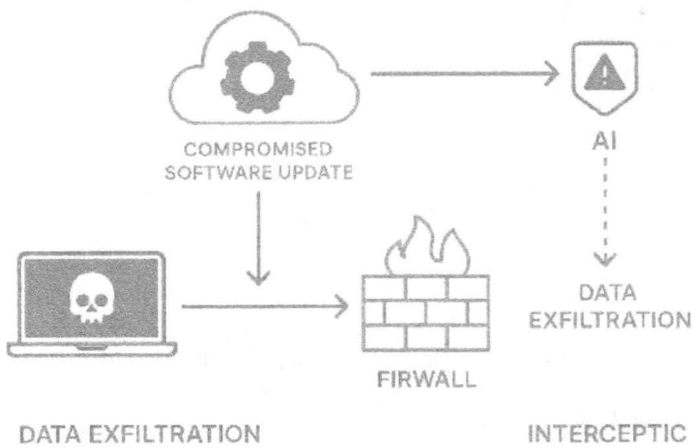

Real-World Example: TrustCheck Flags a High-Risk Cloud Tool

What Happened

A mid-sized healthcare consultancy integrated a new document sharing platform for faster client onboarding. It passed a basic IT checklist and offered great UX — but no one vetted its security track record.

Their AI-enabled vendor monitoring tool, TrustCheck, flagged the vendor within 48 hours:

- The platform had been linked to a recent credential-stuffing campaign
- Public repositories showed hardcoded API keys in its SDK
- The company had no documented incident response or support SLA

The SMB paused rollout and replaced the vendor with a better-audited alternative — avoiding what could have been a catastrophic breach involving PHI (protected health information).

What Went Right

- AI flagged issues the team would never have discovered manually
- Actionable reporting made it easy to justify the change internally
- The business avoided risk without expensive audits or consultants

What We Learn

- Vendor trust should be earned continuously — not assumed once
- AI enables SMBs to act on complex risk signals in minutes, not weeks
- Even small decisions (like choosing a file-sharing tool) can carry big implications

---

Tools That Make Vendor Risk Monitoring Accessible

You don't need a dedicated compliance officer to manage third-party risk. AI-based tools are now affordable and designed for SMB use.

SMB-Friendly Platforms That Flag Supply Chain Risk

- **TrustCheck**: Continuously monitors vendor reputation, breach exposure, and software hygiene
- **SecurityScorecard**: Assigns security ratings to thousands of vendors and offers remediation suggestions
- **UpGuard**: Tracks third-party risk across cloud systems, compliance indicators, and data sharing
- **Panorays**: Offers contextual vendor assessments with automated questionnaires and scoring

What to Look For

- Continuous, not static, monitoring of vendor risk
- Integration with procurement or access control workflows
- Alerts that are easy to understand and act on — without deep cybersecurity expertise

TrustCheck	UpGuard	Security Scorecard
SMB Usability	✓	✗
Cost	$	$$
Alert Quality	High	Moderate

Conclusion

Your vendors are part of your attack surface — whether you like it or not. Fortunately, AI now gives SMBs the same caliber of supply chain intelligence once reserved for enterprise security teams. By continuously evaluating vendor behavior, update integrity, and historical breach indicators, AI helps you spot weak links in time to act.

With the right tools, even small teams can make risk-informed decisions, cut ties with dangerous partners, and reduce exposure without slowing business growth.

Next Steps

Review your vendor list and map out who has access to your systems or data. Deploy an AI-enabled vendor risk platform to monitor reputations, breach exposure, and update behavior. Focus first on vendors with direct access to customer, financial, or health data.

In the next chapter, we'll bring everything together in a real-world case study — showing how AI stopped insider data theft at an SMB, what signs were flagged, and how the response unfolded.

Chapter 8: Case Study — How AI Saved an SMB from Breach

Introduction

AI can feel abstract until it saves your business from a real threat. While previous chapters have explained how AI detects abnormal behavior, secures identities, and defends endpoints, this chapter shows what that looks like in practice — when seconds matter, and a subtle anomaly means the difference between containment and catastrophe.

In this case study, a 100-person legal services firm narrowly avoided a breach that could have exposed client records, litigation strategies, and privileged communications. The attacker wasn't a hacker halfway across the world — it was a trusted employee abusing their access. What stopped them wasn't a firewall or a policy. It was AI.

Background: The Company and the Risk

This mid-sized firm provided legal research and case support to law firms across the country. Their clients included Fortune 500 corporations and high-profile litigation teams. With valuable intellectual property stored in internal SharePoint and cloud drives, the firm had invested in Microsoft 365, endpoint protection, and MFA — but had no dedicated security team.

As business grew, so did the complexity of data access. Contract employees, remote staff, and shared drives became the norm. While the environment was productive, it also created blind spots — particularly around insider activity.

Risk Factors Present:

- Broad internal access to sensitive documents
- Limited audit of file-sharing or download behavior
- No Data Loss Prevention (DLP) tools previously in use
- A single IT manager wearing multiple hats

What Happened: AI Detects Suspicious Data Access

In Q1, the firm deployed Microsoft Defender for Business with AI-powered insider risk detection and integrated it with their Microsoft 365 environment. The system began learning how employees accessed files, logged in, and used internal applications.

Four weeks later, the AI flagged a senior research analyst for unusual activity:

- 800 files accessed in one evening — 10x normal behavior
- Unusual combination of file types: legal briefs, billing data, HR records
- Data transferred from SharePoint to a personal OneDrive, then to a USB device
- Login session initiated from a previously unseen personal laptop

The AI scored the behavior as **"high-risk insider activity."** While the analyst's credentials were valid and the files were not marked restricted, the combination of volume, timing, device fingerprint, and file categories triggered a behavioral red flag.

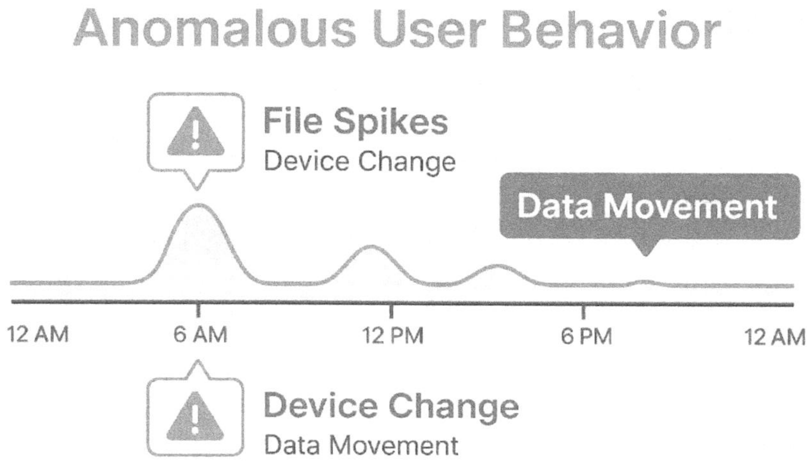

The Response: Fast, Automated Containment

The alert reached the IT manager within minutes. Thanks to AI-generated context, they quickly saw:

- The analyst had been with the firm for three years, with no prior issues
- The flagged activity included non-client documents the user never accessed before
- The session was live — data was still being copied

Immediate steps taken:

- Endpoint isolation was triggered through Defender for Business
- Cloud session was forcefully logged out and access token revoked
- Security team used built-in forensics to audit full session history
- HR was notified and began internal investigation

Later, it was revealed that the analyst had accepted a role with a competitor and was collecting materials in preparation for departure — a classic case of data exfiltration before resignation.

Total incident timeline:

- Suspicious behavior detected: 10:23 PM
- Alert triggered: 10:24 PM
- Session terminated: 10:27 PM
- Data loss prevented: 100% — no files exfiltrated externally

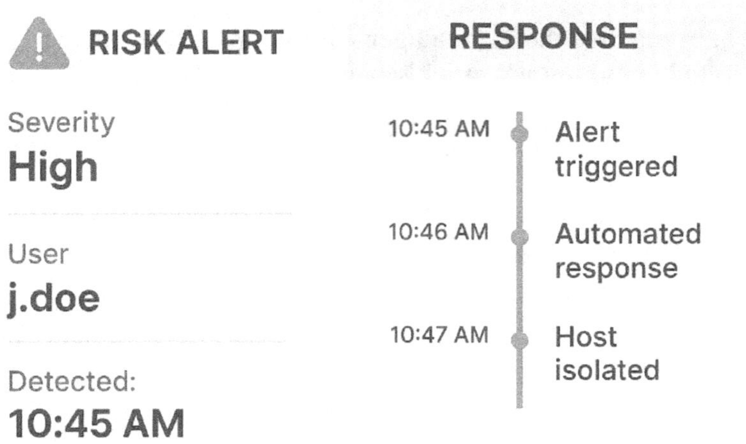

Tools and Techniques That Made the Difference

This outcome was not the result of a sophisticated SOC or an expensive enterprise solution. It was a strategic implementation of affordable, AI-powered tools available to most SMBs:

Deployed Tools:

- **Microsoft Defender for Business**: Behavior-based anomaly detection, automated endpoint isolation
- **Microsoft Purview Insider Risk**: Context-aware alerting across file access, downloads, and movement
- **Microsoft 365 Activity Logs + Audit Trails**: Provided full visibility into session history and user behavior

Why These Tools Worked:

- AI recognized behavior, not just static rules
- Alerts included context: "who," "what," "how unusual," and "risk level"
- Automation closed the gap between detection and response

Key Features Used:

- Real-time behavior scoring
- Cloud-to-endpoint session mapping
- Predefined risk thresholds for sensitive file categories

Lessons for Any SMB

This wasn't a massive cyberattack. It was a quiet insider preparing to leave — and it could've been devastating.

Here's what SMBs can take away from this case:

1. Insider threats are real — and common. Not every breach involves a hacker. Often, it's a trusted team member making a poor decision. These are the hardest threats to detect without behavioral analytics.

2. File access volume matters. Sudden spikes in access, especially outside business hours, are major red flags. AI can spot these shifts in patterns without manual rule-setting.

3. Credentials alone don't guarantee safety. This user had valid login credentials and hadn't triggered any malware alerts. What stood out was how different their behavior was — something only AI could identify in time.

4. Response speed changes everything. The window for data theft can be measured in minutes. AI-enabled automation reduced response time from hours to under five minutes.

5. You don't need a big team to win. With AI-powered tools, one IT generalist can do the work of a full security team — identifying threats, containing incidents, and reporting outcomes confidently.

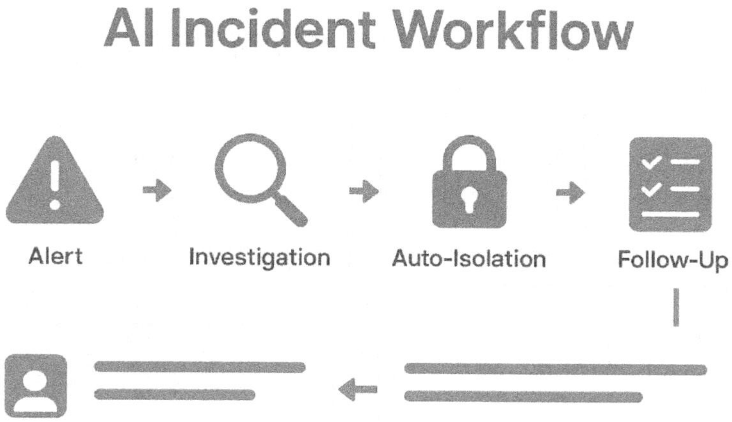

Conclusion

This case is not an outlier — it's a glimpse into the future of SMB security. As more threats come from within, and as IT complexity grows, AI becomes the force multiplier every small business needs. It offers speed, clarity, and decisiveness when human monitoring falls short.

By adopting AI-powered security tools, SMBs can detect threats early, act quickly, and protect their most valuable data — even when the threat comes from inside the building.

Next Steps

Start by reviewing your current detection capabilities. Are you monitoring for file access behavior? Can your tools identify unusual activity from legitimate users? Look into platforms like Microsoft Defender for Business or similar EDR/XDR solutions with insider risk modules.

In the next chapter, we'll examine **the dark side of AI** — how attackers are now using generative tools to launch smarter, faster, and more convincing attacks. From AI-generated phishing to deepfake CEO scams, we'll explore what SMBs need to watch for — and how to prepare.

Chapter 9: The Dark Side — When Hackers Use AI

Introduction

AI is transforming cybersecurity — but not just for defenders. Criminal groups, nation-state actors, and fraud syndicates are now turning AI into a weapon. The same tools that help protect your business can also be used to deceive, evade, and exploit.

For SMBs, this shift is critical to understand. AI-powered attackers don't need to brute-force your systems — they can outthink them. They can write flawless phishing emails, clone voices and faces, generate polymorphic malware that constantly mutates, and scale social engineering campaigns faster than ever before.

This isn't theory. It's happening now. And it's reshaping the threat landscape in ways that demand new levels of vigilance, adaptation, and trust in AI-powered defense.

AI-Written Phishing and Polymorphic Malware

Phishing has always relied on tricking humans — but AI makes the trick nearly perfect.

AI-Generated Phishing

Tools like large language models (LLMs) allow attackers to:

- Craft personalized phishing emails with perfect grammar and tone
- Mimic internal communications using stolen email threads

- Localize attacks across languages and regional norms
- A/B test emails to optimize click rates, like a marketing campaign

These messages are far harder for employees to spot — especially when they imitate bosses, clients, or IT personnel convincingly.

Polymorphic Malware

On the technical side, AI is helping attackers create **malware that changes itself**:

- Each version has a slightly different structure or code signature
- The goal: evade signature-based antivirus and static detection engines
- Combined with fileless delivery (e.g., via PowerShell or browser memory), it becomes nearly invisible to legacy tools

Tactical Indicators for SMBs to Watch

- Sudden increase in phishing reports that sound eerily "real"
- Unusual macros or scripts inside legitimate-looking files
- Malware alerts that disappear on second scan (a red flag for polymorphism)

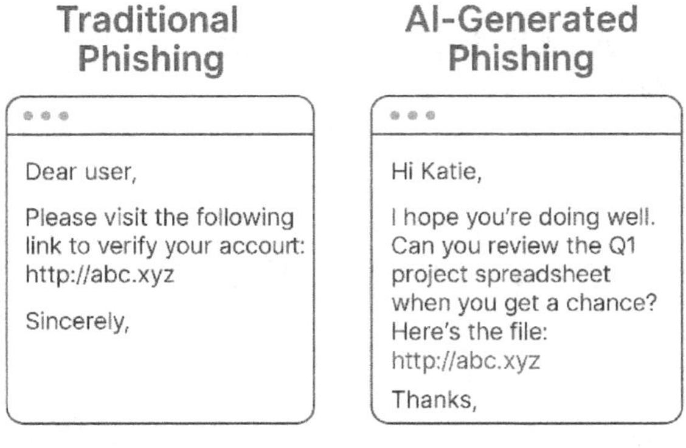

Deepfake CEO Fraud and Social Engineering at Scale

Perhaps the most alarming trend is **deepfake-enabled fraud** — when AI is used to mimic a real person's voice, video, or communication style.

Real-World Attack Tactics

- Voice deepfakes: A fake audio clip of your CEO instructing a finance lead to authorize a wire transfer
- Video deepfakes: Embedded in video calls or presentations, impersonating executives or customers
- Real-time AI impersonation: Using synthetic voice tools to call vendors, reset passwords, or social-engineer internal staff

At scale, these tools allow threat actors to run **mass-customized attacks**:

- Thousands of targeted voicemails or videos
- Personalized spear phishing for every executive
- Fake social media interactions to gain trust or visibility

Key Defenses for SMBs

- Verify financial transactions via out-of-band channels (voice, SMS)
- Train staff to recognize deepfake red flags (odd pauses, lip-sync issues, urgent tone with vague detail)
- Use AI-powered identity and behavioral analytics to verify not just *what* was said, but *who* is saying it

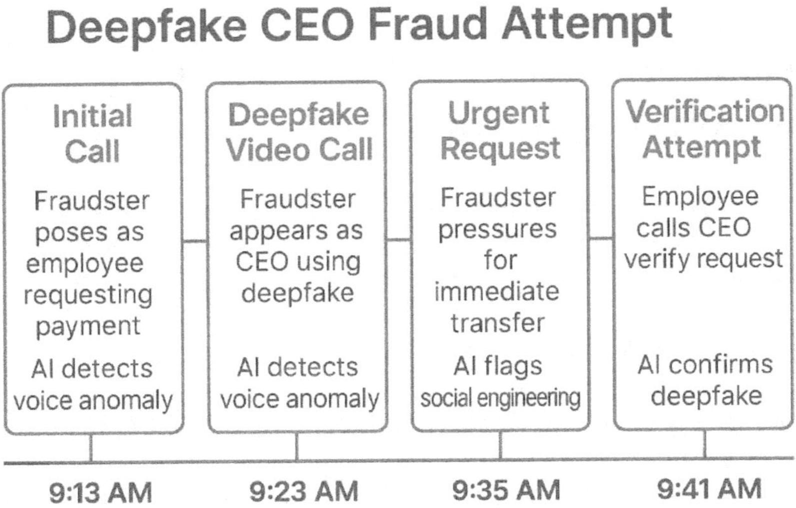

How SMBs Can Prepare for AI-Powered Adversaries

AI may be raising the bar for attackers, but it also arms defenders with better tools — **if SMBs adopt them wisely**.

Checklist: Practical SMB Readiness for AI-Driven Threats

- **Upgrade email security**: Choose AI-native tools that use NLP and behavioral analysis to catch phishing and impersonation
- **Invest in behavioral endpoint protection**: Stop polymorphic malware by flagging how it behaves, not just what it is
- **Enable anomaly detection for logins and file access**: Catch unusual behavior quickly — even from "trusted" users
- **Use verified communication protocols**: Establish known-good channels for financial or sensitive requests

- **Conduct deepfake and AI fraud awareness training**: Short, role-specific training can go a long way

Common Pitfalls to Avoid

- Assuming AI-generated attacks "only target large enterprises"
- Relying solely on employee judgment to detect deception
- Ignoring security fatigue and alert overload — AI works best when paired with streamlined processes

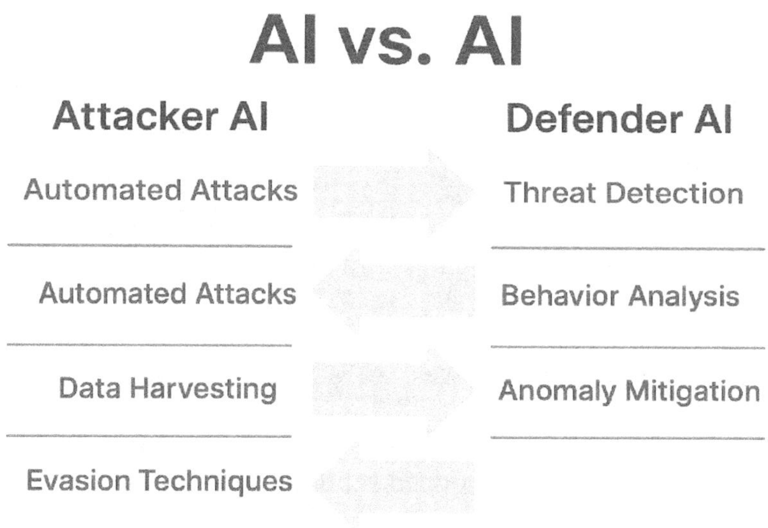

Real-World Glimpse: AI vs AI in Action

What Happened

A logistics company received a phone call from their CFO — or so it seemed — requesting urgent approval of a vendor payment due to a banking issue. The voice sounded real. The tone was calm but urgent.

But AI in their phone monitoring and email platform noticed:

- The number was spoofed
- The voice patterns didn't fully match the CFO's speech profile
- There was no previous reference to the payment in email threads

Their system flagged the event as suspicious and triggered a manual confirmation protocol. The call was a deepfake — and the $70,000 wire was never sent.

Why AI Made the Difference

- The fraud was *technically perfect* to the human ear
- The behavioral AI noticed subtle mismatches in communication history
- A simple fallback process (call-back confirmation) stopped the attack cold

What We Learn

- AI-based attacks are more convincing than ever
- Behavioral baselines and cross-channel verification save the day
- Trust, but verify — and let AI handle what humans can't perceive

---

Conclusion

AI is not just a defensive tool — it's also being wielded by the other side. SMBs that continue relying on static defenses or employee intuition alone are increasingly vulnerable to deception, automation, and scale-driven threats.

But there is hope. The same AI techniques used by attackers are also being used to outmaneuver them — with faster detection, deeper analysis, and smarter decision-making. The key is **adoption** — choosing AI tools that are built for small business needs, and combining them with strong policies and user education.

Next Steps

Assess your current exposure to AI-driven threats. Are you protected against realistic phishing? Can your systems detect behavioral anomalies or flag deepfakes? Strengthen the weak links now, before they're exploited.

In the final chapter, we'll explore **where AI in cybersecurity is headed** — from predictive risk scoring to autonomous response, and how even the smallest businesses can future-proof their defenses without breaking the bank.

Chapter 10: The Future of AI in SMB Cybersecurity

Introduction

Artificial Intelligence is no longer a buzzword in cybersecurity — it's a reality shaping how threats are detected, decisions are made, and incidents are stopped in their tracks. But for small and mid-sized businesses (SMBs), the question isn't whether AI is coming. It's how to **use it wisely**, **trust it responsibly**, and **leverage it affordably** to stay ahead of threats.

The future isn't about man vs. machine. It's about humans and AI working in tandem — machines for speed and scale, people for judgment and context. From predictive analytics that warn of risk *before* it strikes, to autonomous tools that act in milliseconds, the SMB security landscape is being redefined.

This chapter isn't just about what's coming — it's about what **you** can do today to stay secure tomorrow.

Autonomous Response: Faster Than Any Human Can Act

Cyberattacks don't wait. In most incidents, the critical window — the difference between containment and catastrophe — is just **a few minutes**. That's why autonomous response is fast becoming a cornerstone of modern cybersecurity.

AI-powered platforms can now:

- **Detect abnormal behavior** in real time
- **Score risk dynamically**, based on context
- **Take immediate action** — isolate devices, block access, revoke tokens — without waiting for a human to approve

This doesn't mean AI runs wild. These systems are built to **escalate based on certainty**, and many operate in *learning mode* before taking full control.

Examples of Autonomous Actions SMBs Can Enable:

- Automatically quarantining endpoints showing signs of ransomware activity
- Revoking OAuth tokens for compromised accounts
- Blocking malicious links or file downloads mid-session
- Locking out users showing signs of account takeover

Tactical Tip Start by enabling autonomous response for **low-risk, high-volume threats** — like phishing or malware downloads — and build trust in the system before expanding.

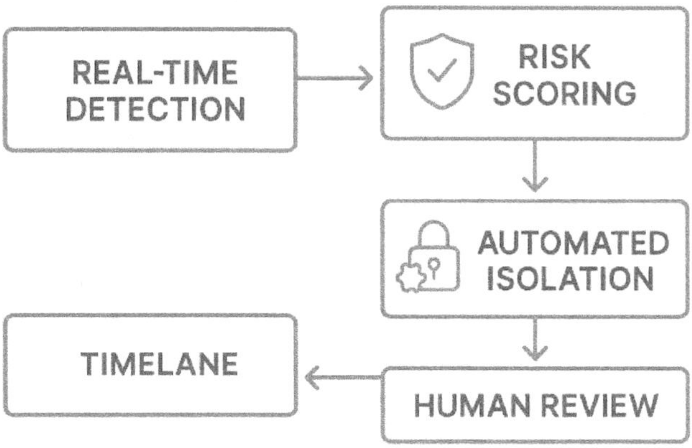

Predictive Risk Scoring and AI in SIEM

Imagine knowing *where* your next breach is most likely to happen — before it occurs. That's the promise of **predictive risk scoring**, now embedded in next-gen SIEM (Security Information and Event Management) tools.

These platforms analyze:

- Historical attack patterns
- Current user behavior
- Known vulnerabilities
- External threat intelligence

They then assign **risk scores to assets, users, and activities**, helping you focus resources where they matter most — not where it's easiest.

What This Looks Like in Practice

- Flagging a third-party HR app with lax controls as a likely entry point
- Identifying a department with poor MFA hygiene as a breach vector
- Surfacing an under-patched server connected to sensitive client data

For SMBs, this means:

- Less time chasing false positives
- Clearer priorities for patching, policy changes, and training
- Smart allocation of limited IT or MSSP resources

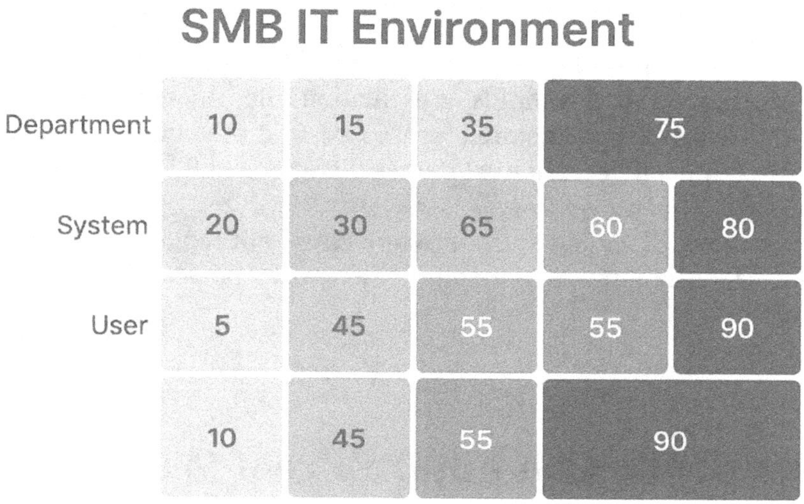

Ethics, Transparency, and Human Oversight

As AI takes on more responsibility, **trust** becomes paramount — especially for SMBs without in-house data scientists or compliance officers. That means vendors and tools must be **explainable, accountable, and aligned with human values**.

Key ethical pillars for AI in cybersecurity:

- **Transparency**: Can you see how a decision was made?
- **Bias awareness**: Is the AI treating different users or roles fairly?
- **Control**: Can your team override, audit, or fine-tune AI decisions?
- **Privacy**: Is your sensitive business data used for *your* protection — not for vendor training or resale?

Questions to Ask Before Adopting AI:

- Does this tool offer a human-readable explanation of alerts?
- Can we set thresholds or escalation rules ourselves?
- How is our data stored, processed, and protected?
- Who is liable if the AI makes the wrong call?

Remember: AI should **support your team**, not replace it. A well-tuned AI system makes human judgment *more powerful*, not obsolete.

How SMBs Can Future-Proof Without Overspending

AI can sound expensive — but it doesn't have to be. Many SMB-friendly platforms already **include AI features by default**. The key is choosing tools that deliver real value without bloated feature sets you'll never use.

Practical, Affordable AI Steps for SMBs:

1. **Start with what you have**
   - Microsoft 365, Google Workspace, and many endpoint tools now include AI risk detection natively.
2. **Adopt platforms that consolidate**
   - Look for tools that combine EDR, email protection, and identity monitoring with AI built in.
3. **Partner smartly**
   - Choose MSSPs or MSPs that offer AI-powered services and help interpret results.
4. **Automate low-risk decisions**
   - Let AI auto-block suspicious links or isolate malware without approval.

5. **Invest in training**
    - A well-informed team can use AI tools more effectively — and catch what automation might miss.

Avoid These Common Pitfalls

- Over-investing in tools you won't maintain
- Underestimating the need for policy and process around AI
- Ignoring user education — the "human firewall" still matters

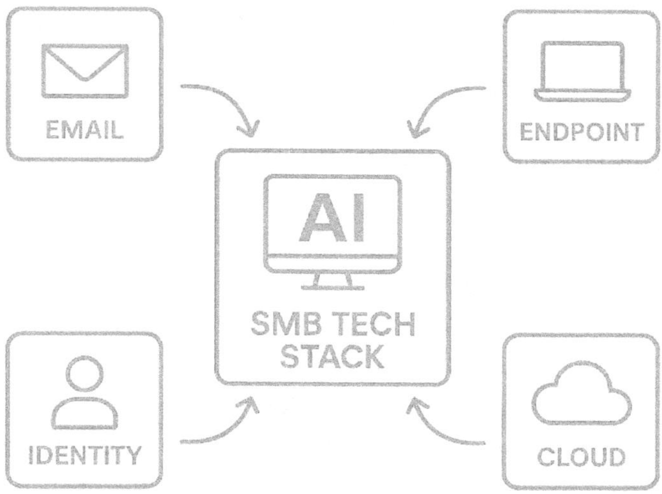

A Vision Forward: AI + Human, Not AI vs. Human

The best future for SMB cybersecurity isn't autonomous or manual — it's **augmented**.

- **AI monitors, alerts, and acts** with precision and speed.
- **Humans guide, adjust, and govern** based on business context and values.

This synergy empowers even small teams to handle enterprise-level threats — without adding headcount or complexity. It's not about replacing people. It's about unlocking **more protection with less friction.**

What SMBs Should Expect from the Future

- **Self-healing systems** that detect and fix misconfigurations automatically
- **Proactive coaching** from AI: "This user is a target — enable stricter MFA."
- **Voice-enabled investigations**: "Show me all login anomalies from the past week."
- **Unified AI dashboards** that combine identity, endpoint, and cloud data in one view
- **Security that just works** — invisibly, intelligently, and affordably

---

Conclusion

AI is no longer optional — it's essential. For SMBs facing rising threats, shrinking budgets, and limited staff, AI levels the playing field. It brings scale, speed, and smarts to your defense — but only if used with care, clarity, and strategy.

The good news? You don't need to predict the future. You just need to prepare for it — with tools you can trust, policies you can enforce, and partners who speak your language.

The future of cybersecurity belongs to those who combine **human judgment with machine intelligence** — and that future is already here.

Next Steps

Take stock of your security stack. Are you using AI to its full potential — or just scratching the surface? Build a roadmap that starts with what you have, prioritizes integration, and focuses on visibility. Choose tools that explain their decisions, not just enforce them.

And remember: cybersecurity is no longer about reacting to threats. It's about predicting, preventing, and preparing — with AI by your side.

Glossary of Key Cybersecurity Terms

AI (Artificial Intelligence)

The use of machines or software to simulate human decision-making. In cybersecurity, AI helps detect threats, analyze behavior, and automate responses.

Anomaly Detection

A technique used by AI to identify unusual behavior or activity that may indicate a threat — even if no known attack is present.

Autonomous Response

Automated security actions taken by AI (e.g., isolating a device, blocking a login) without waiting for human intervention.

Behavioral Analytics

Monitoring how users and systems typically behave in order to detect suspicious deviations, such as strange login times or file access patterns.

BEC (Business Email Compromise)

A type of attack where threat actors impersonate executives or trusted partners to trick employees into transferring money or sensitive data.

CASB (Cloud Access Security Broker)

A tool that monitors and controls how users interact with cloud services like Microsoft 365, Google Workspace, or Dropbox.

Conditional Access

A security approach where users are granted access based on certain conditions like location, device, or risk level.

Credential Stuffing

An attack where stolen usernames and passwords are used to try logging into other systems, betting users reuse credentials.

Deepfake

Synthetic media — usually audio or video — generated by AI to mimic real people, often used in impersonation or fraud.

DLP (Data Loss Prevention)

Tools or policies that help prevent sensitive data from being leaked, shared, or moved improperly.

EDR (Endpoint Detection and Response)

Security software that monitors and responds to threats on devices like laptops, desktops, or servers, using AI to detect anomalies.

Endpoint

Any device that connects to a network — such as a laptop, phone, or workstation — and can be targeted by attackers.

Fileless Malware

Malware that doesn't involve a traditional file — instead it runs in memory or uses native tools like PowerShell to avoid detection.

Insider Threat

A security risk from someone within the organization — whether malicious (a rogue employee) or unintentional (human error).

MFA (Multi-Factor Authentication)

A security method requiring users to verify their identity with at least two forms of verification (e.g., password + phone).

OAuth

A protocol that allows apps to access user accounts or data without exposing passwords — often used in third-party integrations.

Phishing

A form of social engineering where attackers send fraudulent messages to trick users into revealing credentials or clicking malicious links.

Polymorphic Malware

Malware that changes its appearance or structure with each version, helping it evade signature-based antivirus tools.

Privilege Escalation

When an attacker gains higher levels of access than they should — often moving from a regular user account to admin-level control.

Risk Scoring

Assigning a numerical or qualitative value to a user, device, or activity based on how risky it appears — often driven by AI.

SaaS (Software as a Service)

Cloud-hosted software accessed via the internet — examples include Microsoft 365, Dropbox, and Salesforce.

Shadow IT

When employees use unapproved apps or tools (like personal Dropbox or Gmail accounts) for work, often introducing risk.

SIEM (Security Information and Event Management)

A platform that collects and analyzes security data from across systems to detect threats, investigate incidents, and report on risks.

Supply Chain Attack

A cyberattack that targets one of your vendors, software providers, or third-party partners in order to compromise your business.

Threat Hunting

The practice of proactively searching for hidden threats or attackers within a network — often aided by AI.

VPN (Virtual Private Network)

A secure connection between a user and the internet that encrypts data in transit — often used for remote work.

Zero-Day

A previously unknown software vulnerability that attackers can exploit before the developer has issued a fix.

Thank You

Thank you for taking the time to read this eBook. We hope the information provided has been insightful and will help you strengthen your cybersecurity defenses. If you need additional support, guidance, or services, we at AcraSolution are here to help. Alongside our paid offerings, we also maintain a growing library of free resources, including documentation, articles, and practical guides that can bring you immediate value—no strings attached. Feel free to visit our website or reach out directly—together, we can build a more secure future.

— Eric LeBouthillier
Author & Cybersecurity Strategist

www.ingramcontent.com/pod-product-compliance
Lightning Source LLC
LaVergne TN
LVHW022309200926
848481LV00004B/1249